L e a p

The Walt McDonald First-Book Series in Poetry
Robert A. Fink, *editor*

*Wild Flight*, Christine Rhein
*The Clearing*, Philip White
*Burning Wyclif*, Thom Satterlee
*Slag*, Mark Sullivan
*Keeping My Name*, Catherine Tufariello
*Strange Pietà*, Gregory Fraser
*Skin*, April Lindner
*Setting the World in Order*, Rick Campbell
*Heartwood*, Miriam Vermilya
*Into a Thousand Mouths*, Janice Whittington
*A Desk in the Elephant House*, Cathryn Essinger
*Stalking Joy*, Margaret Benbow
*An Animal of the Sixth Day*, Laura Fargas
*Anna and the Steel Mill*, Deborah Burnham
*The Andrew Poems*, Shelly Wagner
*Between Towns*, Laurie Kutchins
*The Love That Ended Yesterday in Texas*, Cathy Smith Bowers

# L e a p

elizabeth haukaas

Introduction by Robert A. Fink

Texas Tech University Press

This book is typeset in Filosofia. The paper used in this book
meets the minimum requirements of ANSI/NISO Z39.48-1992
(R1997). ∞

Designed by Lindsay Starr

Library of Congress Cataloging-in-Publication Data
Haukaas, Elizabeth.
    Leap / Elizabeth Haukaas ; introduction by Robert A. Fink.
        p.cm. — (The Walt McDonald first-book series in poetry)
    Summary: "This eighteenth winner of the Walt McDonald
First-Book-Prize in Poetry explores loss, grief, vigilance, and
endurance. Three sections—Mortals, Lovers, and Mothers—focus
on brutality, death, and other personal or public tragedies from
which the single-mother persona would prefer to turn away, but
instead turns toward and survives"—Provided by publisher.
    ISBN 978-0-89672-647-5 (alk. paper)
    I. Title.
    PS3608.A868L43 2009
    811'.6—dc22

                        2008048166


Printed in the United States of America
09  10  11  12  13  14  15  16  17 / 9  8  7  6  5  4  3  2  1


Texas Tech University Press
Box 41037, Lubbock, Texas 79409-1037 USA
800.832.4042 | ttup@ttu.edu | www.ttup.ttu.edu

For Jonathan, Rebecca, and Emily

# acknowLeDGmenTs

I am grateful to the editors of the following publications in which a number of my poems appeared, some in slightly different versions:

*Agenda*, "Mothers" (retitled "Waterloo")
*Crab Orchard Review*, "Three Odes"
*New England Review*, "The Blues"
*New Millennium Writings*, "The Hummingbird Heart"
*North American Review*, "Red"
*Tigertail: A South Florida Poetry Annual*, "Corrida"
*Tulane Review*, "Red"
*William and Mary Review*, "Firenze"

I would like to thank my teachers, Michael Dennis Browne, A. Van Jordan, Alan Williamson, Rick Barot, and Liz Arnold, for enlarging my world.

I am indebted to everyone at Warren Wilson—especially Thad Logan, Beverley Bie Brahic, Idris Anderson, Jilena Rose, Maudelle Driscell, Martha Rhodes, and beyond measure to Leslie Shipman—for everything.

To the Thursday night group in Denver for whom thanks will never be enough, I express my deepest gratitude to Gail Waldstein, Connie Boyle, Hildegard Guttendorf, Margaret Walther, and Joy Stross.

For keeping me going with their love, laughter, and support, I also thank the Poetry Dogs in New York City: Myra Malkin, Susana Case, and Larry Loeb.

Appreciation is given to my sisters, Catherine Watson and Jane O'Reilly, for their beautiful words.

Above all, I thank my children for enriching my life with theirs.

# contents

xi    Introduction

M O R T A L S

5    Corrida

7    The Hummingbird Heart

9    Red

10    Buffalo in a Snowstorm in Wyoming

12    Baltimore, City

13    Lilydale Tornado

14    When Berryman Jumped

16    Her Children

18    A sound so deep

19    The Morning of the Party

20    Upper East Side Dog Park, New York City

22    I won't tell you

23    Things I Might Have Told My Daughter

24    How We Learn Metaphor

25    Ice

27    Death Retires

L O V E R S

30    Invitation

32    Rio

34    Lake Calhoun

36    Honey Bees

38    The first time you sleep with someone other than your husband

39    Adult Children Survivors Of

40    Firenze

41    Big Surprise

43    The Problem with Being Married to a Foreigner

45    A farmwife in the heartland

46    Why I'm Late to Meet My Husband at Therapy

48 White-Out

49 A capella

50 Drown Out the Sorrowful

52 Lingering

54 Afterward


MOTHERS

59 The Blues

61 Jar

63 Unthinkable

64 The Visitor

65 Waterloo

67 Blame

68 Dust

69 White Tiger

71 Echo

72 Black

75 Cedar Lake Commune

77 Mount Airy

79 The Doctor

82 Garage Sale

Three Odes

    83 No. 1: To MS

    84 No. 2: To Oranges

    85 No. 3: To Bipolarity

87 Territory of Women

88 Bargaining with the Gods


89 *Notes*

It seems fitting that I began writing the first draft of this introduction on Sunday, May 11, Mother's Day. To my mind, Elizabeth Haukaas's orchestrated poem sequence *Leap* is a book about mothering—"the ferocity of love's ministrations" ("Her Children"). The book's arrangement suggests a musical composition's ordering of thematic motifs, dominant at times, at other times subordinate—a reminder they might at any moment reassert their dominance. *Leap*'s three sections—*Mortals, Lovers,* and *Mothers*—develop the themes that compete with each other throughout the sequence, each seeming to demand preeminence, so it is appropriate that *Mothers* be the final section, its thematic motif of "love's ministrations" now acknowledged as the book's dominant theme, celebrating a mother's love transcendent over a carnal, dying world and its transitory pleasures and relationships.

Mother's Day morning in church, I was surprised by our pastor's introduction to his sermon. I was expecting the typical Mother's Day blessing, but he said this is a hard day for many women. *Mother*, he explained, is not necessarily a word with happy connotations. He asked us to look around the sanctuary. He noted that the pews were at least a third empty. He went on to enumerate specific examples of pain many women feel on this day of recognition and praise, but I kept hearing his choice of adjectives—*hard*, and possibly because I came of age in the 1960s, and more probably because I was thinking of Elizabeth Haukaas's persona, her nightmares continuing each morning, each noon, permitting no easy sleep each night, I found myself thinking of Bob Dylan's quintessential song of the '60s—"A Hard Rain's A-Gonna Fall."

I doubt the preacher had considered Dylan's hard rain, but I couldn't stop trying to recall individual lines from the lyrics. When I got home, I looked up the song. I was pleased to discover there seemed a logical connection between Dylan's imagery and my interpretation of Elizabeth Haukaas's persona: Where had she been? What had she encountered on her life's journey through the *middle of seven sad forests*, through *ten thousand miles in the mouth of a graveyard*? Hadn't she met a *young woman whose body was burning*? A man . . . *wounded in love*, another *wounded with hatred*? A poet and his song dead *in the gutter*? What had she seen and heard: A *newborn baby with wild wolves all around it*, . . . *guns and sharp swords in the hands of young children*, . . . *the roar of a wave that could drown the whole world*?

*Hard* is the word for this world, for the life of *Leap*'s persona, and like Dylan's prophet-minstrel, the persona sings the reality of *black* as the world's *color, where none is the number*, and she knows her song well, having earned it the hard way; for her the singing confers its own blessing, its own salvation. Like Dylan's prophet, she will *tell it and think it and speak it and breathe it*, . . . *reflect it from the mountain so all souls can see it*. Now I sound like a preacher, but I don't think I'm forcing my interpretation, my theology, on this book. If we live long enough, all of us will *walk to the depths of the deepest black forest*, and don't we all pray to find our way through, our bodies bearing the righteous scars we have earned? A kind of faith. A moment's triumph.

*Leap* is a powerful book. Maybe I should say *painful*. The single-mother persona speaking throughout the poem sequence has borne more trauma than one person should have to endure, but endure she has, with courage and stamina, refusing to look away from the terror that flies by night, the grief that nests in her life. We can't ignore the persona's pain, sadness, and guilt of hard experience, but the book's title prepares us for more than the leap of Primo Levi throwing himself down the stairwell ("The Hummingbird Heart"), more than the poet John Berryman's leap from the bridge ("When Berryman Jumped")—the leap of death. The title, as I perceive it, refers primarily to the persona's leap of faith, leap of love, despite the probable and the improbable consequences. Rather than a leap of despair, the persona's is a leap for life.

Section I, *Mortals*, establishes from the beginning that the persona will confront Death and brutality, and bravely not look away ("Corrida"). In the poem "Lilydale Tornado," the persona says, "I cannot look," then declares, "I cannot look away." The poems throughout the collection enumerate the public and the personal tragedies from which the persona would prefer to turn away, but she can't. It is her inability to turn her back on Death, in all its forms, that elevates her to almost archetypal status, specifically that of psychologist Carl Jung's *earth mother*, though this is not to say she is not also a dangerous woman, Jung's *femme fatale*. She is, after all, *ferocious* in "love's ministrations."

The book reveals her to be both victim and victimizer, but only in relation to her husbands and lovers, never to her children. For her children, she is the tree planted beside still waters, as she confirms in "The Blues," when she declares, *I'm the mother.* " "I love." The many losses in her life, "the failures of the heart" ("Red"), have taught her that "the line between humanity / and survival" is "fragile, eggshell" ("The Hummingbird Heart"), the line that permits human dignity and grace. Even Death can appreciate such valor, going against his nature by permitting life and even considering retirement, but the persona is ever diligent; she is *the mother*; she knows Death always has "one / last task before his party" ("Death Retires"). She does not sleep.

In Section II, *Lovers*, the persona demands the men in her life recognize love may come, but only if earned, like she has earned her body, "its white / net of scars the medals" awarded for the birthing and nurturing of her children—"Jonathan, Rebecca, Emily, / and the ones / who didn't make it" ("Invitation"). She has borne "the brunt of love" ("Adult Children Survivors Of"), "grief's familiar / gnar" ("Big Surprise"), and yet she can still look for "beauty in the ugly" ("Rio"), show compassion even for a dying squirrel, a *"rodent"* which she hates, when it seems to call to her, *"Human, I suffer. Can you help me?"* ("Why I'm Late to Meet My Husband at Therapy").

Her quest for the permanence of love may be partly explained by "Afterward," the final poem in the *Lovers* section. As a child, the persona needed a father and a mother who loved and protected her, not parents who, though they acknowledged their daughter with "more than / passing mention" in their story, did not consider her "the main event." This is not the case for the persona's children, as the final section, *Mothers*, makes clear.

"Blues," the first poem in the final section, defines the ferocity, the all-inclusiveness of the persona's love for her children, her love for small victories against MS, against childhood diabetes, against "hurt / and tingling" bodies. What this mother loves is "the kind of pain I can fix." She confesses, in "Echo," her need to hold "my children too close," the need unfulfilled by her own mother ("Waterloo," "White Tiger," "Black," "The Doctor"), the need that now the persona's daughter offers to fill, *There, there,* my girl says," comforting her mother ("Echo"). The unthinkable for the persona would be giving up / abandoning a child ("Unthinkable"). She does not give up; she does not look away:

"Knee deep / in murk I try to save what I'd saved" ("Black").

The final two poems in the book define the territory of women: the fecund plain on which the persona battles Death and bargains with God for life. She bears the scars of many mortal combats. Death has been kept at bay: *not this time, not yet* ("Territory of Women"). In "Bargaining with the Gods," she is willing to do anything God requires as she bargains for her daughter's unborn child. She will "sacrifice / envies, desires for the lurid / deaths of enemies"; she will "drop / paper money in the cups / of homeless men." She will forgive her father, forgive her daughter's father, whatever is required of this mother to protect her daughter, to "distract the gods" while she prays for her unborn grandchild, admonishing the "little soul" to "latch on . . . dig in."

"Latch On, Little Soul, Dig In" would have been a good title for our pastor's Mother's Day sermon. He could have spoken this prayer as the benediction before we gathered our things and headed out into the sunshine, grateful that no hard rain was falling, at least not now, not on this day of atonement, its sacraments, its blessing.

Robert A. Fink
*Abilene, Texas*

L e a p

It's no use reminding yourself daily that you are mortal;
it will be brought home to you soon enough.

ALBERT CAMUS

m
o
r
T
a
L
s

. . . all stories if continued far enough end in death . . .

ERNEST HEMINGWAY

It was for the novilladas, the beginners,
The matador, the flourishes,
And the backs turned on death
That I begged my father to take me to the bullfight
The summer we spent in Ciudad de Mexico
As far from the influences of drugs and sex
As he could remove me when I was seventeen
The last summer before I got pregnant.
He went with me everywhere: to the plaza
Bargaining for the silver trinkets for my sister and mother
To the bodega for the cigarettes
He let me smoke in front of him
To the pool where he sat upright, reading,
In hard shoes in the shade as I sunned myself, bored.
For the corrida we had sombra seats, the best,
Sparsely filled. As the sun's orange deepened
Town boys from the gradas came down,
Sat around us, sometimes reaching out
To touch my gringo hair. In the ring, I expected
The pirouettes with the muleta, color against dust.
Not the other red, cascading down the beast's black flanks—
To see the splattered velvets, matador, and hide,
To smell the pinkish foam, the bull's droplets mixed with sweat
When he shook his enormous neck,
The banderillas sinking deep, lodging in muscle,
fluttering vibrantly—I didn't expect.

One of the boys put an arm around me: *No mires, no mires*
He whispered into the air. My father stood
Scattering the boys like pigeons.
He smoothed the creases in his pants, appeared to stretch his legs,
Sat again, closer in the swelter,
Draped his arm across my shoulders.
The bull, front legs collapsed, shimmered,
Silenced, as my father and I were,
By the merciful, now, puntilla.
My father refused to let me accept an amputated ear,
Still warm, held up first to me, then to him,
The gesture for bravery, for not looking away.

Primo Levi watches a man eat
a hard-boiled egg in full view
of his camp-mates, writes
twenty years later of the line between humanity
and survival
that allows a man to remain a man.

Twenty years old, she curls on her bed
moist and embryonic, egg-bald now,
a half-faced girl. Heart beating like a hummingbird's,
she never heard of Bell's palsy. Heard
of leukemia. Never knew indignities,
knows this indignity.

The watertight egg is what prolongs us—
our humanity sealed moist inside the amnion
with our hair, brains, thumbs, and let's not
forget our diseases—
and the same sac saving us
saves the wren, the crow, the hummingbird.

Picture this:
a picture inside a picture:
a girl-baby curled inside her amnion,
her girl-baby eggs safe inside
their own tiny jewel cases
like a set of Russian stacking dolls.

The Russian of Auschwitz, friendly
with the guards, guzzles his hard-boiled egg
yellowing his beard as if with pollen,
lives another fifty years
to write of the larger guilt
of surviving.

A friend—whose daughter's skin is thin
as albumen, whose child vomits food
bland as a hard-boiled egg, whose survival is all
that matters to him at fifty—who now understands
Primo Levi at the stairwell, understands that the line
between what happens to one man and another

is fragile, eggshell.

A bottle of nail polish falls to the floor—
all the crimson of my life reflected in that glistening pool:
copper braids of my third-grade best friend
cut off, delivered in a long box, like roses, after she died;
my mother's lip print on a folded Kleenex in an evening bag,
a smile from her grave;
lacquered Corvettes drag raced to death one summer;
my prom dress unworn, the color of what was left
of my date's foot—who mows the lawn before a dance?
the uterine stain: you're a woman now,
the secret stain when, at last, I was;
cramps that didn't come, the clinic, the slow drain out;
cupid's bow of my baby's mouth
bird-opened for my purple nipple;
dawns I rocked into being, my infant's fontanel my sun,
God; embers under an ash blanket whipped
alive from the barest breath;
in an attic corner, my father's gnarled cherry cane;
my own knuckles gnarling every year I gain on my mother;
relic cars, the two-door coupe in my garage
ordered by my father direct to his door,
keys delivered to his vibrating ninety-year-old palm;
New Orleans velvet cake
just one slice, I'd settle for a sliver;
the failures of the heart; heart failure,
killing my friends, more every year;
my pen bleeding out;
eye whites threaded through with veins;
you, when I tell you we're getting old
and you show me we are not.

In a painting of gray sky, white landscape,
     a disappearing
breed, the only color on the canvas,
     looms small
against the curlyicued gilt frame. It hangs
     centered above

an overcarved table. A decanter
     of port jewels
nearby in the sun. There's a market for this
     painting, and others
of Indian-regaled Appaloosas or soldiers
     on the range

just as there's a market in live human
     parts: kidneys, corneas,
faces. Imagine your heart
     hammering behind
another's ribs, a stranger's lips pulling shut
     over your teeth,

a wife opening her eyes to reveal some
     other's blue depths for her
husband's gaze. Is this how we never
     die? We go on
beating and blinking from body to body, so
     civilized. So different

from the savages who consume whole bison:
     hoof, hide, thigh, entrail,
all sustaining. Blue and gold against flaming
     sunsets, soldiers run
the great beasts down. They die out
     and the ghost

dancers die out, knowing when the last
        of the animals
heaves its last breath, theirs is soon
        to follow. But the buffalo know
only what they know, frozen on the plains,
        vanishing into horizon.

of anthems, banners, ramparts, Poe
face first in the dirt. History's harbor
of slaves—*can you hear?*—their sons'
sons' echoes of confinement

from harbors of no hope, the broke-
hearts of mothers, the beating hearts of babies?
Stitch up aortas, tighten the valves
so boys can be men—

invent the serum for surviving
jungle war so boys can die men.
*Don't say* there's no *Equal Op-por-tun-i-ty*
for City-sons: Thurgood, in a black robe,

rises supreme, another, sublime:
*Eubie Blake, Ragtime Great.* Hallowed be
the first electric elevator that carries
a big man all the way to the top

and the stainless steel cars' *whoosh-rise*
in skyscrapers, like the solid steel *clang!*
of cell doors, comes from factory-sweat,
here, as gangly gang boys fresh

from their corners—where the first telegraph
wires were slung by their great-great-uncles
sweating in the rutted mud for free,
not dumb, not free-dom, where Poe's

streets burned to their guts and the slums
of the emancipated rose up—
where boys in their first incarcerations
stare at the ceiling, turn into men.

Arms outstretched, a child's dress
floats from a tree.

We roll down the street
so slow and heavy
I feel the snap of every stone.
My legs stick to the seat.

I close my eyes,
the stones are bird-bones breaking.
This is my father's idea of a Sunday drive.
Later, I learn twelve people died.

With every caved roof his excitement grows,
bigger now than the all day trip
up north where a fall blizzard
left a hundred cows dead (hump upon hump
        of black back cresting the white).

Here, Pompeii at suburbs' hem:
bread on plates, spoons in soup bowls.
Someone's front door yawns,
its upright frame invitation to walk

straight through to nowhere.
My father churns the engine.
I am his willing companion
on aftermath tours,

anticipation shimmering:
I cannot look, I cannot look away.

The bridge that time of year was barren,
A gray throat with no beginning or end.
It was snowing. I'm sure

I wanted to be high. My fingers must have burned
From cold. A rock in my chest
Where once there were ecstatic beats

—I'd been gone so long. The Mississippi
Separated me from my longed-for
Life, the other bank, the peace-freaks and drunks,

Skid row and free stores, the Triangle Bar
Where the underage and ancient mingled,
Ignored each other, smoked, snorted, guzzled,

Injected their pleasure. It was a Friday.
In three days, the new term would begin. Imagine
Me, a coed. Memories disappearing of the boy

I would have died for—if he hadn't beaten me
To it. I'd turn twenty that spring
When T-shirt and bong vendors spread their wares

In tepid sun amid whiffs of sweet home-grown.
My dead lover will always be twenty,
our own boy outlives him.

I should remember what happened next.
Was there a sudden flurry,
People out of nowhere at the railing:

*Did you see, did you see,*
*Someone jumped.* Could I have been
Thinking about the poet at the same moment

He waved to the gawkers on the banks
And they waved back. I wish at the time
I'd been able to say, *if only*

*You'd lift your head from the snow blown deep and soft,*
*Unyielding as a woman, you'll breathe in*
*The bitter air.* But I didn't know the difference then

Between a leap and a fall, a girl at one end
Of a long bridge, despair at the other, that I, too,
Blamed my father for everything.

wait for the ferocity
of love's ministrations:
songs for the deaf child,

for the blind one, sea-
colored blankets;
the diabetic boy comes

home to meringue temples,
an arboretum of cakes;
a child, no longer

walking, is shown Swan Lake
where one hundred legs
cascade across stage.

She tries out new fathers
like slippers. Asks the deaf
child to listen for rain

on the roof, the blind one
to watch for cracks in the sky.
Clouds blister, white fruit

splits, and even senseless
children understand bare
hangers in the closet, tinkling

like chimes. An orchestra
of rattles, radios, talking dolls
for the barren-eared, for the

empty-eyed, walls of sunset
drawings. She pushes a trike
up and down the sidewalk;

the pedals whir like windmills,
limbs hang, limp as flags.
Spring comes, as if

she could mend cave-eyes
aimed at her, silent ears
cocked to her touch,

sugar in the golden stream.

its swells barely rumble human eardrums.
The long low notes stream: a blue whale calling
through thousands of miles of sea. Far off, another turns around,
swims to death for love. You click into hard news, drift off

in a chair at your daughter's bed. The *rat-a-tat-tat* you know is war
sealed in the TV over her head floats in your dreams
into the mouth of a jay. The one who woke you every morning
at her age as you lay waiting for bluer skies, some other bird.

Her chart notes: patient hallucinates. Blue iris
on her walls talk to her: *watch out for flowers*, they say,
*swallow this and this and this.*
You want her back and she takes you back—are you the only one

who sees it, that flicker behind her iris?
You think you'll find the song that turns her illness around,
hum into the prow of her ear a three-beat hymn: *em-i-ly, em-i-ly*.
Somewhere in the ocean of her brain, she hears.

What I remember
of the slow-motion minutes
after the call is the butter:
yellow rivers oozing out
from under its bulk, as I squeeze
the phone between my ear
and shoulder, *yes, officer,*
sidestep to the refrigerator,
plate of butter aloft in both hands
as if it's a lit-up birthday cake,
*yes, red Dodge,* worry
I didn't specify "red wrapping paper"
I just told you "wrapping paper"—

if I had known would I
have lingered longer
on the freckles,
that explosion of pigment
on your arms under the gold
hairs flaming up
in this morning's sun
or touched your face
across the table I haven't yet
cleared of breakfast's detritus,
your crumpled napkin,
the burned ends of your toast?

The day after,
the dogs need to go out.
You hinge their leashes to their collars,
startle at the life fluttering in their necks—
your dogs are exactly as they were
yesterday: eyes, tongues, beating hearts, fur.

You have shape-shifted into the city
itself: a burning skeleton, a protean brain
that conjures the skyscrapers like phantom
limbs, makes whole the people
in stairwells, takes them off the sills,
runs the film backward.

The dog park is full for a Wednesday,
too many men on the benches.
Their dogs don't question this good fortune,
run madly until they can't lift their heads
for another ball, or a new dog, or
what raised their hair an hour before.

For a while the air is just air—
a promising September sky.
Moving up river, majestic plumes of gray-white
open and fold over themselves
as they rise. You realize: smoke, not cloud,
as you breathe in the ash they carry

that yesterday was skin and desire,
organs and voices,
hunger and bones,
as you swallow bits
of three thousand human beings
as you would rain

and you touch the arm of the stranger
sitting next to you, something ordinarily
you'd never do, the particles drifting down
until a sudden shift of wind
blows the ash from your shoulders,
the leaves into fence corners.

why I couldn't welcome you here,
     to eat cake
with your sisters or what kept me
     from letting you
slide into place behind them.
     Don't hold it

against me who didn't even know you,
     I was busy then.
Your cells did their jobs—
     blunt nubs
mushrooming from your seahorse body,
     your bobbing head,

blueberry eyes sealed tight,
     the tendrils
of your mysterious sex—forgive me.
     Why you weren't
here raking last fall in a plaid jacket,
     cherry coins

on your cheeks, you and your sisters,
     dirt on your knees,
when the bushes were sticks and the yard
     slick with leaves—
forgive me. Your paintings aren't taped
     to the walls, your name

in capital blue letters. I won't tell you what
     it might have been,
why there's no lock of your hair
     in a box—
forgive me there's no cake for you,
     no birthday.

When I look away, forgive me.
You're allowed to hate
Any gods you've called on.
Don't be dainty:
Blame the muscles
Choking your arms and legs.
Blame the ridiculous
Distance to the bathroom.
Blame me.
But steady yourself on other arms,
I can't always be there.
It's backwards, I know,
My buttoning your clothes
After all these years.
On the days you can't find the cane,
Find the cane.
And suit-up,
You're a warrior
On whitewater:
Grab stumps, rocks, branches
At the bend,
Another arm.
I can't always be there.
Indulge a lover but remember:
Warn him about me.
If you find someone
With imagination,
Caress him;
If you can't,
Have sex. Have a baby.
Then, just once more,
Take my arm.

My daughter at nine comes home from school
with an assignment to draw her family
tree. *We'll need miles of paper,* I say, *and boxes*
*of crayons. You are one of three by me,*
I explain, *though each of you is an only child.*
We unfurl the roll of brown paper, mapping back
to the ear-jarring tongue-numbing Norwegian
names, our ancestors spreading across butcher's
wrap like stain. Connect Bertina to Lars to get
Mangus, Lars to Anya to get Solveig, Anya to Olav
to get Sven. My own past comes honestly
as my daughter prints my name in a square, draws
sunrays outward from me to account for back-seat
groping, coupling in the commune, days and weeks
of real love: Bruce, Dan, Andy. She links me to her
daddy with rivers of blue lines, then, in black,
runs a single hairline tributary downward
to the paper's bottom-most edge. *Stop,* I yell,
*save room for you.* I tell her the family delta
depends on her, she's our headwaters. Elaborately
she S-curves the line, ends it with a tiny bud
resembling drawings at nine weeks or twelve weeks
of disembodied fetuses, their umbilical cords
trailing off to nowhere on gynecologists' walls.
She says, *No, mom, I'm Australopithecus.*
My daughter at nine knows her Lucys,
her Neanderthals from her chimpanzees. She makes
no mistakes when it comes to life's tree, who
dies out, who walks out. At nine, she hums
and colors the boxes of family, their fates long
sealed, unnatural harm years away, still out of her hands.

A filmstrip of your life is supposed to unreel in front of you.
Mine did not.
In fur-collared gabardine coat and matching leggings,
a late-February shortcut
over the pond. Missiling down, the instinct
not to drown
sent me flailing up, the panes of ice
immovable.
An eternity of leisure: floating face forward
against rugged hard.
Where was my birth-memory?
That swift trip
down the canal so fast I'm born in a police car,
my first lullaby sirens, screaming.
Or my parents: surely once there must have been
tender gazes,
the lingering hand on a cheek?
Or prophecy:
in my husband's dream he chased me across some frozen
Nordic cove
but I broke through, a clean descent until he pulled me
back by my hair.
We divorced anyway—years away from the girl's slow
bobbing, lips bluing,
blue eyes open in frigid murk,
the hand-over-hand
toward that tiny sun, my grateful lungs.
This part of the film
plays again and again: crying the whole cold walk home,
the beautiful
coat with matching leggings stiffening,
a body cast.

How they laughed when I burst in, then ordered me
for being late
to the pantry to eat alone in that cool
tomb of preserves.

After eons, he opts for the gold
watch. Years of meeting quotas,
he's starting to repeat himself:
brick-hard dirt and dry skies,

the skeletal tribes of Darfur.
A couple of gods dangled among
the Semitics and voilà, they take care
of things themselves. Filthy English,

some rats and *the great dying*
ensues. If he jiggers the earth
he can take his pick: quakes,
tsunamis, the evaporating smoked-

corpses of Pompeii. The thrill
is gone. He misses the personal tragedies.
Besides, he's gotten soft, lets a plump
three-year-old stay with her mother

one fall morning, inflates the airbag
when he could so easily not. Unwraps
the cord from the neck of a couple's
blue-baby, secretly basks as the tiny

boy inhales, pinks. He could have done
without the smirk on the doctor's face—
*give a little credit where credit's due—*
but he's old, on his way out, a relic.

The mystery's fading on the front
lines where Science encamps, garnering
all the attention. Death dreams—*yes,
Death dreams too*—of a cove

and a cottage, Life's random
pileup. Just once he'd like the look
of recognition when he steps out
from under the dark eaves

to be a welcoming one—*let me take
your cloak, sit a while*—but he has one
last task before his party, before
he reaps his own enscripted clock—

L
o
v
e
r
s

Earn this body.
Dunes of breast, coppery

haloes big as plates now,
they deserve celebration.

My jellyfish belly, its white
net of scars the medals

of Jonathan, Rebecca, Emily,
and the ones

who didn't make it. Worship
what this body knows.

My ragged pelvis, a curved shell
around the long deflowered

darkest part of me.
Give it a hand for staying

on the job. Loosen your tongue
from mine, trace the blue

loops of vein on their overland
journey up my legs. Marvel

along the way at the silent
fireworks, the purple sunburst

new this year. A gift
for you. Don't think it's easy

wearing this body I've worn
so long as if it's some present

you've given me. I'm warning
you: earn this body.

Then, maybe,
we'll talk about love.

Hump of black mountain
in the background—
Sugarloaf? Sugar-sweet-something reigning

over shanties festering
on hillsides, dug into the barest
smear of soil,

rounding rocky edges the way kudzu
rolls over skeleton cars, up phone poles
in Appalachia

where, even with their missing teeth
and banjoes, the indigenous
have it easier than here. I want to see

Bishop's Santarém:
beauty in the ugly, but a woman
squats and shits

in front of me on Ipanema.
I was almost
inside my hotel. It's the fall

before we split up, though here it's spring,
not quite Carnaval.
We don't know yet, under

our umbrellas ordering Schweppes
from the boys with coolers
running up and down the beaches,

trailing the long last *ess* of the bottled tonic
we order, with whatever they put in it
that makes us fawn all over each other

like the rich old men on blankets
still straining their thongs
with such young girls,

that in a few months the house
will be for sale. That when we go back
to our room in the Copacabana,

take off our robes and shower, unlock
our watches from the safe, don
seersucker to enhance our tans,

click the wavy bricks hand-in-hand, make
love at three a.m. and again
as the hillside shanties start to seethe

and the promenade below our window
fills with dawn joggers and beggars
that it will be our last—

That the mangoes and caipirinhas
and the blue and red rooftops
and smell of roasting cashews

and your fingers on my face
will be lost
and all I think I'll remember of that

last trip will be the woman
soiling the black and white tiles
lovers stroll.

From our bedroom on the third floor
of this house of starting over
I have a clear view of the lake:
the sprawl of ice-fishing shacks
to the far shore

where the sputtering lights of the houses
of happiness, abandonment, argument, or love
stare back—
beyond them, stark-lit
freeways heading, always, away.

The ground is hard as a bell,
the grass frozen needles. Here,
all sounds are cold:
the crunch of cemetery paths yesterday
as I stomped around

looking for my parents, my uncles:
the governor, the boxer, the shyster—
my father referred to them as big dumb
Norwegians. Who's laughing
now, since I married one,

and my father's sleeping
head to head with the whole lot of his in-laws,
forever. Finally, I found
my best friend, the first of our class
not to die in a car wreck.

My husband crawls into bed
behind me, after his arctic bath:
a vigorous rubbing
naked at the sink with a rough damp cloth.
I forget, as I warm him,

the promises I've made
in whispering calls
to another,
to leave, this time
for good.

Marriage is an old man's foot.
Love? Just another bunion.

Children are the silvering under-
side of the infinite illusion. A house

is nostrils, all flare and sensitivity.
In the garden under last year's

trampled plumage, green shoots
reach out in search of a foothold.

Weeding is marriage. Thistles
bloom beautiful, supine and deep,

their purple spines are guilt.
Guiltless, they'll joust with anyone,

blood is blood. The children's
laughter is stars, reflected in red,

it's also temptation, albatross,
the igloo's hearth, the fish's

heart, a thousand harps, or wasps
in court. The judge is age.

The parade at a gallop, the ticking
watch, the seasons' sultry

unfurling, bloom, bristles, buds,
plums again. The high octaves

are children, almost out
of range, their decibels

the bells that blue the hillsides,
the rhymes. Love is reason.

Going on is no reason at
all. The bill is all that's footed.

You are empty shoes. No honey
bees, no money on the trees

in the backyard. You know
what money is. Money is love.

## THE FIRST TIME YOU SLEEP WITH someone
## OTHER THAN YOUR HUSBAND

all you think about is ninth-grade dance class:
*let the boys lead, dear,*
and how the boys' collars smelled
like cellars, how their still
soft palms dampened your starched
blouses, how you
became this woman: one hand over your abdomen,
ribbony from childbirth,
as you shutter
the blinds with the other, wondering if he's ever
slept with someone your age—
When it starts, your fingers wander down
his back seeking
the hollow held together by a scar, a red
zipper sealed over
his spine, fused so he could lift his future
children—only there is
no hollow, no scar, and *this* man will move
nimbly out of bed
in the morning without looking back to make sure
you register his pain—
Here in the immediate dark, his strange
gentle snore warming
your neck, you forgive him for being nothing
like the man
imprinted on you, how *that* man
was forgotten
for one fiery hour.

It's not your mother's fault. She's sitting
on the silk dining room chair in 1969
staring at her glass, its amber
contents lovely to her as she lifts the razor
thin crystal to her lips.
It soothes her like a mother's hand on a forehead.
Or your father's,

as he sits alone at the kitchen table,
baseball on the radio,
when you steal your way in.
He hears you. Calls out to you.
And you know the beginning and the end.
His drink is aubergine, the color you'll paint
your foyer four decades later.

But that summer night, as you stand
on the creaking back steps
unblinking to shrink your acid-gorged pupils,
shouting *good night* through the wall,
you are so young.
Your mother goes silently
up the front stairs to bed

as your father fills a glass,
brings it to you, holds it to your lips
and asks if you *do it* how it *feels* if you *come*.
Night, the alcohol, the dope, the dolorous tones
of your father above the ball game
no one's winning or losing
offer little escape from the brunt of love.

An idle afternoon's snack brings it on:
I cleave an apple on the cutting board,
lay open the white flesh,
reveal two Tuscan suns.
Dew rises to the wound's surface.
Light gnaws at the edges,
sears an ochre membrane.
The fruit goes a little sweet with air.

That summer, we sliced apples thin as leaves,
dropped them as we would tablets
into dense berry-black wine. We fished
the soaked sheaves out with our fingers,
sucked the slices white again,
back to pure apple,
stained each other's skin with purple lips:
two pale halves exposed to being.

That the one you loved most
was worst. Jonquils came up
in February in New York this year,

scarves of yellow doomed
by the snows that would come
in March. As if you were fooled

into thinking it spring, like beards
on bald men. The day you come home
to find he's left with everything

you own, except the connubial
sheets, what can you do
but pull them up over your face,

disappear as you wait for someone
to notice. A holiday of time
to blame the dead. Then you're standing

at your father's bed, the only sound
in the room the green bleat of his heart
machine. Over and over you turn

this scene in your head as if
you'd actually been there, leaning
close for his final words, a bona-fide

goodbye, a fare-thee-well.
The mind's cutthroat map catapults
from death vigil to wedding, your last

one, the World War I of marriages
both of you agreed, your Ken and Barbie
smiles full tilt, linked arms akimbo.

That your mother attended the blessed
event to say it would never last—no,
it would be her last—pink scarf

at her throat hiding the pinker scar.
That your father said, *why bother,
they'll be others*, and your parents

argued like children: *you're selfish
I hate you I hate you more*. After
forty years with her he doesn't last

the year without her. The year
your beloved splits your lip
because he loves you, you love

him more. That your own heart's
thrum gnaws at your eardrums
and your lungs puff and deflate

predictable as tides until, alive
enough to recognize grief's familiar
gnar, what can you do but scream.

*Pick up some artichokes,* I say.
He comes back with avocados, ripe and warty.

He says *delicatessen* for delicacy,
*eat-your-heart-out* when he means
*eat-to-your-heart's-content*—

· A clever bon mot fails
this man whose feelings consort
with the hard consonants slamming together
in his mind, some fiery otherworld

he can't express to me.
I say, *I hate you,* he merely agrees
as if he were a customer service rep:

*I can see you must be frustrated
by my complete inability to meet your needs.*

I say, *I love you.* He says, *Jeg elsker deg.*
*But why,* I say and my Viking becomes the child

in the photo on his desk: post-war boy,
home-knit sweater, foot on a soccer ball,
lighthouse eyes on the person behind

the camera he says was his father.
A rare weekend home but he missed
his boy's match. That same look now
for me, the settling. He doesn't say:

*We're done with all that—*
*the leaving of each other.*
*Why do you love me,* I say and say and say

and he says, as if words could explain it,
*Because you are my delicatessen.*

whips up breakfast for the field hands,
dogs sniffing at the back door for ham
bones and potato skins, as the TV beams
disaster into her yellow kitchen much as the sun
streams through last century's tall double-hungs
whistling like sirens from the ice-laced winds,
but her husband when he's home on leave
will caulk the glass, then he'll fix the splintered
porch stair that could swallow up a man's
leg, not nearly as bad as the towers in New York
left the bones of men in splinters so miniscule
no one would know they were human
but bad enough for her to make such
connections of men gone for good, their wives
remembering the creak of his boot on a step,
the way he'd lift the hair from her neck
to kiss her there—she knows she's blessed,
full freezer, matching divans, sodded prairie
to every horizon where she and her husband
when they were just kids stripped
to their underpants, crawled through sumac
on their bellies hunting lion, pretending
it was Africa much the same he tells her now
in his letters how he belly-creeps between
jeeps, pitiful-skinny dogs at his heels, sand
blinding as North Dakota sun on snow,
he'll be home soon, *darling*, she can almost
hear him say it as she hears the gravel
crunching in the driveway as the official
army detail winds its way past the elms,
their dingy ribbons whipping in the wind.

Absorbed in the task
of chewing off his front foot,
twitching on my sidewalk,
he doesn't startle until he sees me
out of the corner of one mad eye
and flops like a hooked fish on a dock,
jaws firm on the forepaw
he thinks he'd be better off without.

Someone else wandering by
would say this squirrel is dying:
*Let nature take its course,
it's a rodent.* But then its eyes focus:
*Human, I suffer. Can you help me?*

I hate squirrels—
ever since one leapt out of a tree into my hair,
digging his black hooks into my skull
deeper the faster I flailed. This squirrel too
is rank with fear, but harmless,
busy with death.

Three paws clawing sky,
he's on the lawn now, on his back,
his own blood on his lips a lipstick-grin,
glimmerless eyes.
He's still.
Flies begin to darken his hide.
I move to cover him with a box

and he flips suddenly over,
cloaked with grass clippings.
He burrows into the yard's green fringe
as if to make that sweet-familiar,
not danger, or pain,
what he'll take with him
into the permanent dark.

There are reasons to go
into it, nature busted loose on 86th Street,
vertigo at the door
of Walgreens: the raw, the howl,
the bravery.
The anonymity. And your pills are low.
Out of the white
vortex, dark forms materialize,
float larger toward you,
a Macy's Parade of memory-cartoons
you think
you recognize. There he is, your last lost
lover. You hang
onto a signpost, still yourself
in the swirl. He bobs forward, his frozen smile
not his. Weather does this,
this hope-hypnosis. You let go the sign, stomp
onward, hands balling
the lists in your pockets, wonder if
that swerving taxi
jumps the curb, blasts you into some
unknown aurora,
will the crumpled paper you leave behind be enough
to identify your body:
*White-Out. Shampoo. Plaquenil. Glue.*

Cave of you: pulse of lungs,
the snaking throat,
the heart's squeeze, release—
you pray to them, your new

gods, though you're mundane
as yesterday, which is not
to say without amends.
No frosty breath at your back,

you still want a new sofa,
red. At least your blood
is honest week to week,
but apparently amnesiac—

can't recognize
good guys from bad—
so you step off the curb
and your ankle jellies:

who to give this news to,
this Eve's apple? Your too-
young lover fails to deliver
comfort other than himself

oblivious as your dogs
who eat, shit, sleep, tremble
in their dreams of a wild
they never had, never will—

you lie awake, your life real.

## Drown out the sorrowful

after Yehuda Amichai and Louis Armstrong


Dress me when I die in high heels.
Dress me in my merry widow.
Fasten the garters and for God's sake
cross my ankles, cock my head.

Curl my lashes 'til they shadow
my cheeks, powder my lids with blue,
blues thumping in the background
when I die. Let my daughters loose

in my closet with my dresses,
my boas, my feathered hats.
Let my perfume wrap around them
as they laugh and cry in turns,

inhale me deep. Let them choose
the jewels I'll wear for God—
When the sun comes up again
let my husbands have a hand

at arranging me as they please.
To the shotgun one I say:
*Feast on the black lace beneath,*
*so sorry my breasts are ice,*

*my lips sealed, I can't wink.*
*God we had it good on the porch*
*summer nights breath-hot.*
To the peacock I say:

*Zipper up my skirt, button up*
*my shirt, don't let me go out*
*underdressed for death.* I say
to the swing-shift: *you grew*

*to be a bore, nothing more.*
But to the last, the heart-smasher,
the one who left me, I say: *Why.*
Close the lid, gather together

at the river: harps, tubas, daughters
with their cheeks stinging,
the men I loved standing pat
in straitlaced boots. Let them

all feel the heft of my body
sealed in mahogany,
before what's left is ribbons, cirrus,
song.

Toward the end I wondered
which time would be the last
time. Every few days, one
of us forgetting, our arms opened
for the other, until inevitably

morning. And the wretched
recognition in the blank face
of the other emptied of accusal,
empty as the graves of our children,
a girl, a boy, unborn.

Years before in Café du Monde,
so late, or early, even New Orleans
was tucking in, we agreed
to correct a mistake, preserve
our freedom—*It* would ruin it—

but in Rome a year later, where
we went on a whim, did I lie, was I
careless, did biology kick in?
With pregnancy still small
as a bullet, certain this time

he'd say, *yes, let's go ahead,*
the perfect moment became a fist
to the stomach. Not literally,
of course, though he threw his shoes
first one then the other at the wall.

Hands on my shoulders, he tried
to shake the baby out of me,
though that one soon died on his own,
like the marriage, irretrievably.
Our babies would be five and six:

*pick up sticks*. I see them together
at the corner, cornflower eyes,
hands locked as they look both ways,
their delicate frames taller than the rest
in line for the school bus.

Admit it, even when the windows
rattled with argument, in the mornings
cream was poured and you ate your
sweet cereal. Admit it wasn't you,
not even you could console her.
Or raise her from the bed, bring her
out to the garden to see what you saw.
You were happy, admit it, to let
the years of serrated silences
as you ate in front of the evening
newscasts tumble by. Until you could
at last leave man and wife
to themselves and advance your own
feculent plans for a requited life,
admitting no part of the father, mother,
child of the house of shattered
plates aimed at love's ducking
head but hitting, instead, the walls
in bursts of yellow fragment. Admit
you miss what you heard of love's
scald. His pleadings to be
let back in, the fires in the hearth,
the short hard thumps
of bed frame bumping floorboards
before the thudding out, the door
slam. You've got to admit both
times you stared down at the still
face, the fist-tight eyes and sutured
mouth, first hers, a few months later
his, that what you remember
wasn't love's facsimile and what you
think you've forgotten was never

the child's to know. You figure
somewhere in their story, more than
passing mention, but not the main
event. It was the mother, her skin
against the father's, and the father
whose large hands stroked her hair.

m
o
T
H
e
r
s

Dilantin, depakote, copaxin, keppra:
I love the small square room
where my blue-gowned daughter
sits on the exam table, swinging her legs
because this week she can, which is why I also love
prednisone, a little.

I love this doctor even though he asks who I am.
I say, *I'm the mother,*
so he'll know we're on equal footing
here as my daughter, between us on the narrow
sheath of steel, kicks up a breeze.

I love the tuning fork
he touches to her skin as he asks if she can feel it
*there* and *there* and *there*
as much as I love the rubber hammer
he runs along the bottoms of her feet.
I love that today her toes curl
downward in response, in MS-defiance,

the way they should, the way I loved
blue on the strip in the jar of my son's pee
and the forty cc's of insulin
I injected into his bony arm every morning.
I loved when that was the worst thing
ever to infect my family

except when the dog had cancer
the summer before and we had to put her down,
all of us crying over that hound—
I love the kind of pain I can fix
with a new puppy. Ambien, Valium, Xanax:

I love the darkness they bring
as much as I love the days beyond
these walls, my daughter
supple, mobile, able, Ritalined, Avonexed,
bruised—I love her bruises, the golden hues,
the blues, the full spectrum of old blood
and new, mingling inside her hurt
and tingling body—

the body that's still here.

jar

The calcite half-moons of your nails,
your static lashes, your bald scrotum
all useless as

your umbilicus drifting to the top of the jar
to the space between lid and liquid
as if for air.

You'd be fifty-five, you'd have had
years on me. The story goes, your mother
stumbles to a hospital, delivers two blue boys

too fast to sober up, leaves empty-handed
unlike the doctor who attends to you:
my father (ever god-alert when he drinks

Dewar's in his crisp white scrubs).
They say you aren't viable
though your twin breathes long enough

to bury. You, they would have wrapped
for the trash in a paper blanket, incinerated,
had my father not preserved you:

the almost-miracle. All these years floating
safe and deaf in your mason jar womb,
formaldehyde cradling you

on the back of a shelf at the back of the pantry
with shoe polish, varnish, a tray of rusting
vein-clamps. Be glad you were uncontaminated

by living. Be glad he let you be.
Now the ocean around you is clouding,
a leak in the seal. You're disintegrating

as fast as my father, who no longer
knows he is a doctor, or has a daughter
but this isn't my story, little immortal

suspended in your glass tomb,
it's yours, as if any of us
or what we do endures.

—the creature squirming
outside her belly at last

would not change her
mind, that she could let

him root blind
as a mole into another

mother's soft flesh—
unthinkable, yes,

even eleven years later
as her boy, mad

for an unknown father,
kicks holes in walls

and she dreams
what might have been

for him, for her,
had she let the nurse

lift him glistening
placenta-wet, hide his face

from hers, disappear
down the dark hall

she runs toward,
her arms empty—

You open the door. The lake-eyes
of a still-honest blonde stare back.

You know her,
the half-moon scar on the cheek.

Memory on your threshold in the shape of a body:
your body, seventeen.

You welcome her in, set another place,
so many stories to swap:
> *In a year you'll be a mother.*
> *He'll marry you and leave.*
> *It's your son who breaks your heart.*

Broken glass clatters from her throat.
You've forgotten you ever wept so unabashed.

What is she doing here, unstitching
your past:
> *You think you love him, the first one.*
> *You'll remember that night I promise.*
> *But, baby, could you reconsider?*

Tell this child across the table
about the little boy she'll drag like a sack

from man to man. That when she opens the sack
to mother the boy she'll find

only moth husk and snake skin.
Put your arm around her young shoulders,

whisper what's in store at her own hand.

Old songs loud on the radio,
mopping my own floors one Saturday
years after she's gone, Charlie Faye
materializes: *child, you know*
*you can't come home with me—*
to where her real daughter, Ivory,
the baby in her locket, lives.

I dress my cat, wheel it in a buggy
so she'll see how good I am with babies
but Charlie Faye's family
stays mystery: *they my* co-*leagues—*
when I beg the names of the women
in gray dresses and sponge-soled shoes
who ride the city bus with her,
peel off into side yards. Their chatter
flutters under the cathedral arches
of the bridge on mornings I hide,
watching for the school bus to pass
so I can slide down the scree
to river's edge to kill the day.

As if she were my mother,
Charlie Faye's wide cackle when I come in,
her mouth the inside of a poppy.
*Lemme fix that hair, missy,*
*like you was at school today—*
rebraiding it squint-tight.
Then: *Outta my kitchen, Chinky—*
one lung long lost, the other
a bass drum that summons my mother:

*Really, Charlie Faye, we don't slur*
*the races here*—and I learn
the evil eye. Flecks in her irises glinting gold
as her teeth, Charlie Faye glares through walls
into bridge-playing wives as smoke
from skinny cigarettes furls from their mouths.
I ask what my mother pays her:
*it's more'n adequate*—

to make the tiny sandwiches
that curl on trays at the elbows
of the ladies in our dining room,
to love me from seven to seven
Monday through Friday. Charlie Faye claims
a husband too: *checkered, he is.*
*Gone so long he don't know 'bout Ivory*—

I ask to see baby-Ivory's picture
and slip a photo of me
into the locket's empty half.
We smile side-by-side, almost like sisters,
or the angels blazing in the windows
of Charlie Faye's church the afternoons
she takes me with her.

I launch notes in bottles for places
down-river, Waterloo, Dubuque:
*Ivory's daddy took off with a crew*
*for Waterloo*—as far and exotic as Tahiti,
full of men like Charlie Faye's husband
(later, I come to know on my own).
Flame in her eye-whites, her face a cloud
the last morning she cracks our back door:
*Ivory's run off. Eighteen. Jus' eighteen.*

god and brain lesions, electrical charges,
the frontal lobe's void they try to jump, fail, raining sparks
inside my daughter's brain like the raw ends
of a severed power line and blame
the paralyzed face afterward, its blank beauty
stuck there in its most terrible
a minute, a day, they can't say but roll her on her side
so the tongue of taste and love
won't slide down her throat, let it subside,
sponge her off and drive her home, she won't remember
what slammed her to the floor, horrified you
as the sapphire eyes rolled back and she danced
there on her back, the grace of those long legs,
delicate bones rattling the afternoon
and blame MS, the seizure's sinister twin
patiently eating its way through her gray matter—blame
the gray matter—what matters now is *now*,
let's talk quality of life and how it was only mother's milk
for a year, then homegrown beets, handpicked eggs,
no preservatives no sugar no TV no toy guns,
she had dolls and trucks, play kitchens and stethoscopes,
the equality of it all, even now, as her illnesses spar
for which muscles to convulse and which ones to stiffen
and this drug keeps her still and this drug keeps her moving—

Beyond the roof of Norway, in this jagged green bowl,
I find the bone-white headstones:
sentries of the dust, wormed-wood of my ancestors.
My grandmother comes from a second son—
these hills could never have been hers.

Go back a hundred years: steerage, stagecoach, her shock
at the new world's grasshopper-plain.
My grandmother, barefoot and bareback on a nag in Ontario
minding scrawny cows, her mother recovering
from childbirth ten summers in a row.

The seething brittle droughts of fall: the little girl charged
with littler ones. Her mama said she couldn't blame *a little girl*
when the baby died in his basket. Never asked, *how?*
Besides, in eight months a new son would squirm
against the tatting, take up the fallow name

and soon outgrow its embellishment: second-Ed.
The parents would eventually be buried in the Canadian prairie.
A tiny slate tilts in sight of their twin slabs,
all three blown smooth by time: I've stood at those graves too.
Now imagine me in their steep homeland—

the edge of a fjord, my grandmother's ashes mixing
with the ashes of the tape she left me, a tinge of accent emerging:
. . . *the house was sod. It was dry that time of year, yellow dust*
*'til you couldn't breathe. I knew first-Ed was dead*
*from the hammer got thrown at his head when papa . . .*

Except for being very rare, the white tiger
is no different from the orange.


Want is what separates me from my mother.
I want the deepening

in her eyes, their candles flaming
when a beloved

enters the room. Our shoes, polished, in a row
by the pantry door

from smallest to largest every morning, the way she lined
us up for pictures,

the girls in identical jumpers, the boys' blue blazers
too loose or too tight.

In the outside world I learned: the high held notes of a diva,
a newborn, a jazz horn,

cabbies' horns, that breath is the soul's true container.
Not skin, not bones.

When it comes down to it, the difference between
fire and ash.

Night's ghostly hand on my forehead—
is that what's left

for the dead to do, spy on the living? A big har-de-har-har
as they tickle us,

watch us twitch in our dreams, the kindling
of memory

primed for a match. Fear is what separates me
from my mother,

my clammy palms, hard-thrumming heart,
lost reasons

she had the nameless faceless one torn out.
Was one of us my mother's

white tiger, the one she'd save in a nightmare?
Would she

have died for *me*? Paced the front porch, gone back
into a burning house?

In bedrooms decorated as if their lives
depend on it, my children
rip each other apart.
How those harp-string chords in their throats
must vibrate as they hurl epithets:
*toad-breath, road-kill—*

As if she were not memory
*my* mother appears, leaving her echo
to the hospital walls,
placing her hand on my cheek.
As if she were more than bone
I hear a *there, there—*

On the floor in the morning
the blue silk robe she wore her last days home.
Even before she died
I took it from her overnight case
for its hint of lily, her expensive scent.
Silly to have packed it—

A hole in my son's bedroom door.
*No idea how it got there*
says the boy, knuckles scabbed,
standing in a halo of sunrise
the room's new porthole extrudes.
My daughter, hair combed, has made her bed—

*I can fix it*, she says. And I think
I must scare them
standing there in my mother's old robe
holding my children too close.
*There, there*, my girl says,
*it's just a door.*

1.

Progeny of nonbelievers,
I dress in black, dream of cloisters,
marrying God—
kneel my knees bloody.


2.

As if they were fruit spilling exotic seeds,
buses burst kids from strange
neighborhoods onto our playgrounds.
We close in on one, snatch

at her hair, laugh and run away.
She calls for her mama
the way we would call for ours.
Shame embers in our bellies.


3.

Bovine floral women, their arms
great flabby wings, descend on my best
friend the year we're nine, the year
her mother went to bed

and never got up. Rouged women
tell my friend her mother's gone
to heaven. I tell her she's in the cemetery.
A year of black. I worship grief.


4.

Spindly queen of junior high nights,
five years from motherhood:
eyes ringed with kohl,
lips a perfect scarlet *O*.

5.
Maybe for the turning away
three times, the picking and choosing
from six hundred commandments,
or the confirmation

from those who should know
there really is no hell, or for the men, or that
they finally let me in
with my blue eyes, Norwegian skin.

6.
Life Drawing. African-American male.
I charcoal in cheekbones,
abdomen, hard thigh. He brushes by
after class, smaller off the dais.

7.
College boys whose names we won't
remember sit on the floors of our black
rooms, smoke blocks of tarry weed.
Black-and-white TVs flicker Vietnam

as we blonde-girls-in-dashikis paint peace
signs black as jungles we don't imagine,
where boys whose names we'll never know
die in living color.

8.
We argue as the sky goes pink then gray,
as we blow on our coffee, into our receivers
at our desks, until we have nothing more to say.
There is nothing more to say.

9.
Cancer sucks the color out of my mother.
Delirious with power, it shrinks her
doll-size. In a final morphine haze
she declares herself a believer, after all.

Dressed for eternity as for a cocktail party,
hair restored to its black cloud, pearls—
my years of practice fail. I forget what to pray
and cry as a child: *Mama open your eyes*.

10.
Cardboard boxes bob like life rafts
in my flooded basement. One by one
they saturate and sink. Knee deep
in murk I try to save what I'd saved.

By October I know the combed wool,
the twist in my fingers as if my fingers
leave lines in the air where I wave them;
hue of molten goldenrod and wool,
blood in the crook of a finger
the taut warp brings; the fleshy rise of dough
warm as a plucked bird—

the plucked bird itself I stuff
and cook and serve to strangers
I call my new brothers and sisters
seated at my table at six o'clock as if
they've come from a hard day at the office—
the hard punch into the dough's belly,
the slap on the counter;

the walk through purple rows of cabbage,
dirt raining from a yanked carrot,
rains that flatten then glisten
in lakes where fields were;
scrub of new food, occasional bug;
the lotus position, *om*-ing
at water's blue edge at both edges of day;

nursing babies one after another,
people who eat the placenta,
people who bury the placenta,
people who pass the babies back and forth
(mother's milk is mother's milk)
sharing their babies like drugs
or lovers;

the witching line to the bathroom,
the dirty tub, stepping over the full
and lazy men loose-limbed on the floor;
asking who's got rent this month, knowing
it bought the maryjane drying in the oven;
broken fingernails, braids unbraided
rippling past my waist;

the woolly clouds, the grasses,
the red-dust path to the road,
the thumb, a sign, a destination;
cold, for the first time, a different hunger
and boredom on the bleached horizon—
a long unraveling.

You shuffle along as if you're one of them—
you could be
after all these days. You're herded
to Arts and Crafts,
which today are ashtrays and potholders,
where you pick from the bins

enough lengths of white and blue
to keep cool
the pot handles of all the therapists you know,
a little memento
of this time with your daughter who intently
presses bits of pink

jagged tiles into plaster she's smeared
in a concave
metal mold. You see how easy it would be to chip
away at a vein
with those pink bits until they're red. Your daughter
smiles at you

angelically—*Some of these people will never
get out,* she says
as a man down the hall lunges at walls,
his straitjacket
tied tight so he won't bite off his other thumb—
you never mention

why she might be here. You skip group this afternoon,
make your muffled way
back to her room where the bland steaminess
of food trays
fills the air and you feel a brief normalcy
in your hunger.

Your daughter's cup of pills precedes the delivery
of her plastic
silverware—*I'm ready to go home, Mom.*
You say, *of course,*
as if she were a child as you fold her cuffs carefully
back to avoid

their dragging in gravy and press flat the bandages
buckling at her wrists.

1.

Sees only their eyes as he skins
their white retinas. They wake
blinking at him, god of sight.

At home he is the fat king
of a bountiful table ringed,
like luminaria, by his obedient children.

2.

But his daughter signs away her child
before it's born. He hand-delivers handicraft:
jigsawed puzzle pieces fall face up, jagged

fragments of a blue-eyed cherub. Unsigned
letters: *Beware the white-child you see on the street,
it might be yours* in his familiar script.

3.

Her mother dies and her father slides
down the proverbial hill. He naps
on benches in the park or artfully,

as if debriding a wound, carves
crusts from hard white bread
to feed the birds. When she finds him

his eyes light up as if with recognition
of a different life: *Your mother and I
are going to the lake. Do you need money?*

4.

The cufflinks in his white stiff sleeves glint.
His daughter's womanly waist, the swish of her skirt
raise a metallic taste in his throat.

5.
The daughter wonders what her mother knew.

6.
It must have taken hours in the basement white-
gluing the Gerber-baby photo to a block of wood,
jigsawing the wood into elaborate shapes.

But it was the newly breathing body
in her arms that changed his daughter's mind
and kept that child, his lifeline, from him.

7.
She's smiling in all the black-and-whites,
pointing at Mount Rushmore or posed at the edge
of Grand Canyon. He snaps his still little girl

in an eyelet dress, pointed shoes, grown-up hairdo.
Her brothers play off frame, throw rocks
at the rock walls, oblivious of ricochets, echoes.

8.
The first time, he rouses his daughter
from the white-deep sleep of a child. Later,
she knows he is there before he is there.

9.
The girl makes up a life for the baby in the jar.
Safe in her closet she unseals the lid, recoils
from the smell as she would from a slap,

reaches in, caresses the parchment skin
as it whitens from air. She makes up the life
she would have for herself.

10.
The father's words, disembodied in the dark,
slide over her, tongues, flicking. In the mornings
he looks up from his newspaper,

over cream and coffee, like a father.
But when she finds her own young lover,
he weeps as a child betrayed.

This curved tin cave, the bread inside soft
as cake. These red chairs, where good
children sat straight at this spackled table.

The clamor, screen doors slamming, dogs
in yards. This Midwest sky, a drop
cloth under real sky. There must be blue above.

Behind this garage, fingers with shredded nails
under a shirt, the smokes, the someday talk.
Thinning light and sound a sure signal

to stop. The quick tuckings-in, the furtive
walk home as if fingerprints glowed. Someone's
little brother covered by a sheet, his body

a pillow on the curb, his missing shoe
found in the street days later. A neighborhood
battened down by hit-and-run, the door-to-door

hustle of women familiar with death,
its protocol. Polished silver, crystal on buffets,
*come-in-come-in* flooding the vestibules, funerals

are parties too. This ostrich-feathered dress,
a chartreuse swoop down front stairs, pirouettes
on the landing. Highballs before the guests,

instead of guests, glass shards in the rugs
mornings after, the missing husband
the father. And the stacks of paperbacks:

*Forever Amber*, *The Carpetbaggers*, *Candy*,
*Fanny Hill*, hidden in parents' nightstands
to save the children from such fiction.

The brain blooms gray-white,
its spiny stalk branching out below
twice, then twice again, each end
a delicate splay, a dexterous plume
of muscle, cartilage, neuron, bone.

Commands filter through
the narrow filaments: *raise the hand*,
or *sing*, and the tongue trills
its lovely notes and the shoulder
lifts the arm and the arm, the wrist,

and so on, until the fingers
flutter through air, until day
no longer follows night. Unyielding
darkness decays the body's
spores, scatters dendrites like seed

husks. Desire's idle thought:
*see the chair across the room, walk
to it* becomes a need, and then
implacability. Still the legs
stay still, resolute. The cleft body

petrifies, though tremors rustle
its branches. Without instruction,
axons aimlessly drift in dark hollows
of the brain's trunk, widening
the distance between body and chair.

No. 2: To Oranges

A housewife stands
at her sink, in her hand
an orange, rind resistant
as skin. A vial of insulin—
opposite of *vile*
its homonym—a haystack
of syringes,
the needles sharp as needles,
are arranged for practice.

Deep inside her own
boy's body, buried deep
inside his pancreas,
the Langerhans islets, once
plump jewel-cases of fuel,
have shriveled, their ducts
the cold smokestacks of a defunct
factory, its facade eyelets
of broken windows.

A drop of sweet, the yield
of one attempt, seeps through
the wound. The orange
never winces. Any mother
can inject one. She stabs
the orange again
and again, until
all the sweet is gone,
no little boy in sight.

No. 3: To Bipolarity

Cans of iron-stiff paintbrushes,
walls half white, half black, bare.

You memorize every wing of the Met,
echo grand-plans daily through its halls.

Only to repeat six months in bed,
your hotline calls greeted by name,

dirty hair and dirty room, the pills
befogging, focusing, happy, hindering.

*It's a good day to die*, you chant,
*I want to live forever.*

No groceries in the house,
you buy a hundred oranges.

Checks bounce, why not
adopt two Persian cats;

you all eat out of cans.
One day you vacuum the rug

eight hours. Affect effectively drug-
flattened, you've found an outside job

filing: two weeks, the same alphabet.
You miss believing you can fly

until you believe you can fly, and
dive into the Hell Gate tides

from the East River cliffs. Before you sink,
seizing-up in cold panic, you soar.

The authorities pick you up
and lock you down.

The mammogram:
vaguer than mass, more ominous.
A mother's long dying,

treatment a poisoning, a body-ambush
as thousands of cells rush in
only to die themselves—

Your own hard pea:
pearlizing invader, genetic traitor—
ever notice how lymph

rhymes with nymph?
You feel fine
then you feel it

one night greasing the creases,
a grain of sand in an oyster gland.
How long has it been there?

A skeleton emerges
after all this time, all that
forsaking of cake for salad.

The raw ridge
you finger under your arm, a tidy slit,
its braille message: *not this time, not yet* . . .

I bargain with God: the god
I don't believe in, the just-
this-once-god, the god

who's already had a field day
with my daughter, for her unborn.
Let the floating sac attach,

let the embryonic Jell-O
grow valves, vessels, its sex.
In the shower as I lather my hair

I am my most pure: I'll sacrifice
envies, desire for the lurid
deaths of enemies, I'll drop

paper money in the cups
of homeless men, I'll forgive
my own father—hell

I'll forgive my daughter's.
Then, while I distract the gods
with my false bounty,

latch on, little soul, dig in.

"Hummingbird Heart"—Primo Levi, the Italian writer and Holocaust survivor, died after throwing himself down a stairwell in 1987.

"Buffalo in a Snowstorm in Wyoming" is how I refer to the untitled George Smith painting I bought in Jackson Hole.

"When Berryman Jumped" refers to the day in January 1972 the poet John Berryman jumped off the Washington Avenue Bridge, which connects the East Bank to the West Bank of the University of Minnesota. I was walking across the bridge at the time. Much later I learned he suffocated in the snow that cushioned the fall.

"The Morning of the Party" is for Kirk.

"Firenze" is for Walter.

"The Problem with Being Married to a Foreigner" is for Stein.

"Bargaining with the Gods"—Madeleine Elizabeth Huffine was born December 19, 2007. She is healthy and beautiful and brilliant.

Selected by Robert A. Fink, *Leap* is the eighteenth winner of the Walt McDonald First-Book Competition in Poetry. The competition is supported generously through donated subscriptions from *The American Scholar*, *The Atlantic Monthly*, *The Georgia Review*, *Gulf Coast*, *The Hudson Review*, *The Massachusetts Review*, *Poetry*, *Shenandoah*, and *The Southern Review*.